For the children of Hammersmith & Fulham   HM

For Beau Henry Wiltshire AG

With thanks to Georgia Bateman, Wendy Dormer and Oliver Gillie

First published 2015 by
Dinosaur Douglas Books
6 Davisville Road
London W12 9SJ

Text and illustration © 2015 Dinosaur Douglas Books
Dinosaurdouglas.com

Printed by PrintHammersmith, 152 King Street, Hammersmith, London W6 0QU

ISBN 978-0-9928759-1-6

DINOSAUR DOUGLAS
HAS FUN IN THE SUN

Heather Maisner

Illustrated by Alex Godwin

Consultants: Kingi Aminu, Consultant Paediatrician at Chelsea & Westminster Hospital and
Kate Barnard, Consultant in Paediatric Dentistry at Chelsea & Westminster Hospital

Dinosaur Douglas is having fun,
Playing with friends out in the sun.

His eyes are bright, he's feeling fine,
Vitamin D makes Douglas shine.

But in the dark, where his cousins play –
All night long and throughout the day –
On TV, XBox, ipad, phone,
The dinos ache and frown and groan.

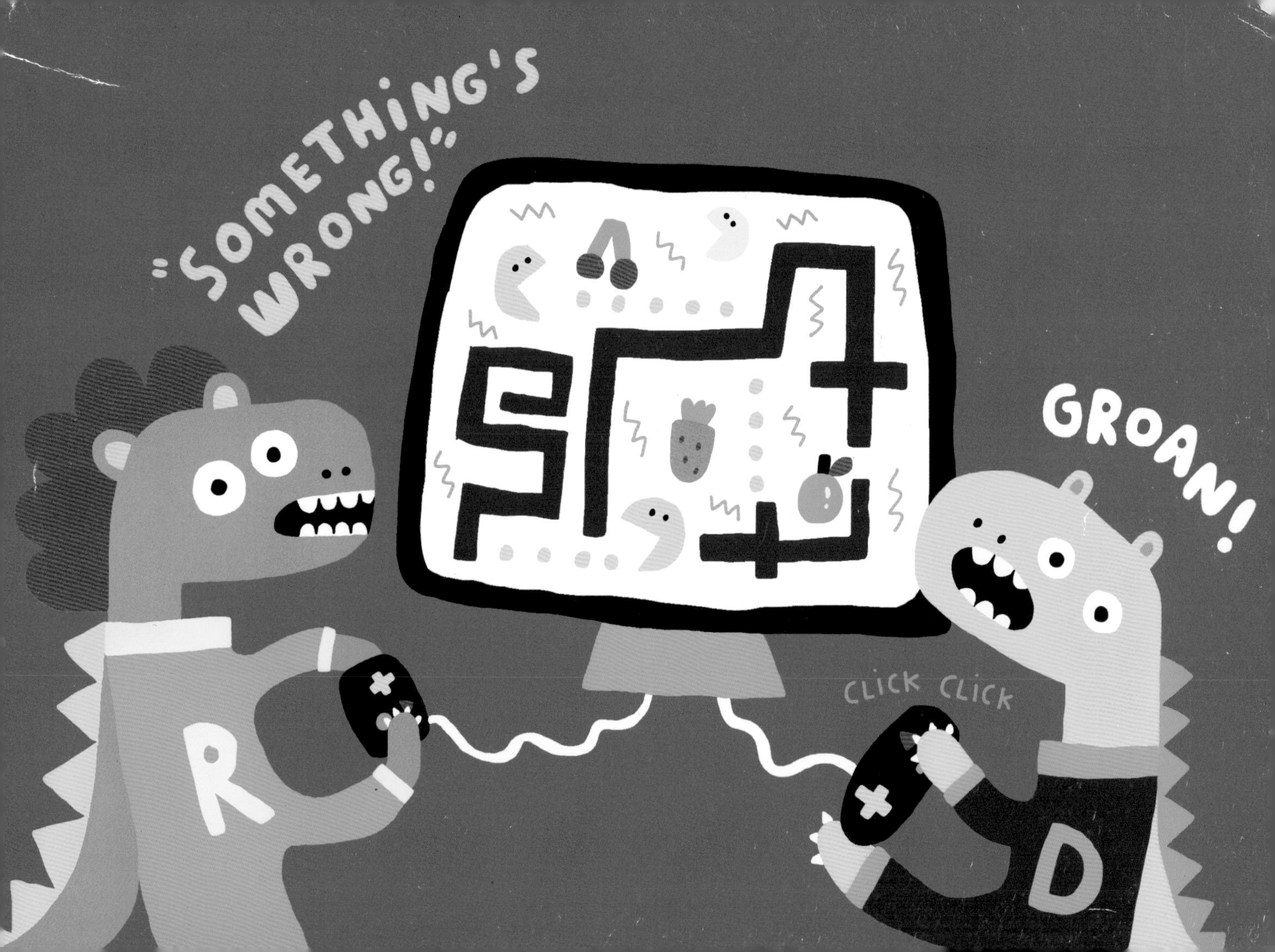
"SOMETHING'S WRONG!"
GROAN!
CLICK CLICK
R
D

Dino Tim is pale. Dino Rosie's frail.
Daisy's teeth don't grow. Danny's legs all bow.
They can't stand up. They can't walk straight.

They don't eat well.
They're losing weight.

In this dark place that has no sun
The dino cousins all look glum.

Something's missing, something's wrong.
"My cousins need to grow up strong.
Help me, please," says Dino D.
"They need to find some Vitamin D."

Out in the yard, can you hear cluck, cluck?
Follow the hens and follow the duck.
Collect the eggs up – one, two, three.
Eggs are full of Vitamin D.

CLUCK

CLUCK

On the beach, slippery wet,
Help the fisherman empty his net
Of oily fish straight from the sea.
Oily fish have Vitamin D!

Open the window, look up high.
The morning sun is in the sky.

Run outside, as quick as can be.
The sun is full of Vitamin D!

Stay outside as long as you can –
You never know, you may get a tan.

But whether you are dark or fair,
Check out what you need to wear.
And when the sun is very hot,
Run and find a shady spot.

And when the weather's cold and grey,
When everyone stays in to play,

When there is no sun in sight,
A vitamin pill helps put things right.

Now the dino cousins are having fun,
Playing outside in the sun.
They have strong bones.
Their teeth have grown.

They've put on weight.
They're walking straight.
They're eating well and happily –
Because they all have Vitamin D!

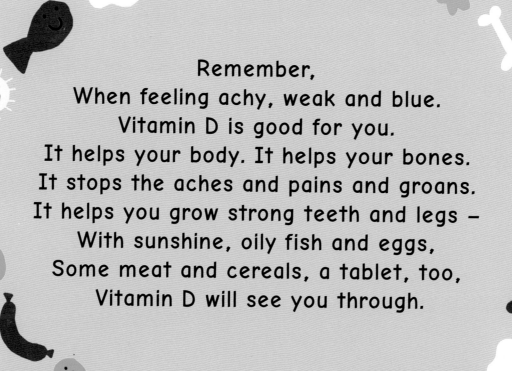

Remember,
When feeling achy, weak and blue.
Vitamin D is good for you.
It helps your body. It helps your bones.
It stops the aches and pains and groans.
It helps you grow strong teeth and legs –
With sunshine, oily fish and eggs,
Some meat and cereals, a tablet, too,
Vitamin D will see you through.

"Vitamin D for me!" says Dino D.
And his cousins all agree.

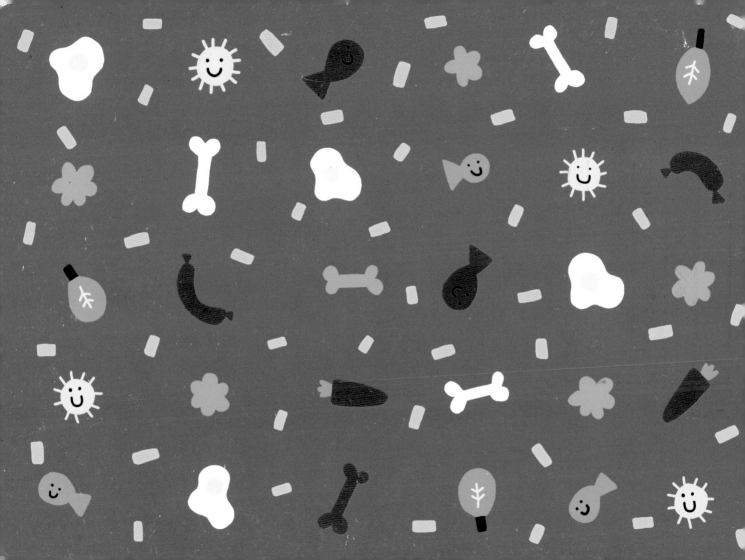